P. M. GENIUS' GUIDE FOR CRITICAL INQUIRY

NATHAN COPPEDGE

PERPETUAL MOTION GENIUS' GUIDE FOR

CRITICAL INQUIRY

Based on a Proven Psychological Method

By Nathan Coppedge

NATHAN COPPEDGE

FORE-NOTE

NATHAN COPPEDGE

Inquiry is often seen in a critical light. But the real inquiry is that which occurs in our own minds. If inquiry has this intrinsic, psychological character, why is it that people want to reduce it to something analyzable?

The answer is that people want to understand their own lives, Not, I believe, out of an impatience for it to end, but instead, because inquiry is a search for the meaning of life.

This book does its best to answer some of the basic questions of existence, using a minimal standard that involves explaining the four dialectical circles through which we all pass.

Far from explaining life away as a process that will someday meet its end, I feel that life is a process that applies equally to the immortal. Keeping that in mind, the book is meaningfully open to new processes of life that may be longer-lasting.

NATHAN COPPEDGE

GUIDE FOR CRITICAL INQUIRY

NATHAN COPPEDGE

INTRODUCTION

Many people undergo a critical process of inquiry during the course of their lives. Whether a person is wise or foolish, brave or timid, pioneering or lazy, people touch on many of the same themes as they undertake development. The goal of this text is NOT to provide abstract tools for reasoning with, but instead, to explain many of the factors that each person eventually experiences in his own mind, in order to make it much easier to tolerate. Thus, the goal of this book, like previous books in the series, is a psychological one. And, it is also a meaningful one.

Now, on to the main text:

NATHAN COPPEDGE

The first dialectical circle occurs in infancy. It is something which takes place in a single room. The room is taken to be the whole world. It is, for this reason, the most serious thing. But it is also very open-ended. During this time, the infant develops the ability to critically inquire, so far as is ever possible for him or her.

1. What is this? Is the first question. To which the infant receives an immediate answer, which may be pleasant or unpleasant.

2. What is me? Is the second question. The answer to this is often more satisfying, unless something has gone terribly wrong.

3. What do people do? Is a third question. And rationally or irrationanally, it becomes answered. The answer may be as simple as the texture of the doctor's gown.

4. Why me? Is the fourth question, and is answered with the best comprehension possible. The baby decides if it is a victim, if it is destined for greatness, if it has a special advantage, and so on, in this fourth moment.

At some point the child undergoes a process of maturation, leading to more practical questions. However, as the infant likely predicted, these questions are not very easy. And they carry problems of their own.

1. One is obsessed with how things are. At first one may not want to know how things work. This stage passes very quickly for some children, but for others it becomes a lagging obsession. Some people dwell in this area as though it is the entirely of their lives. They're not very bright, but it is not that there is nothing on their minds. In some ways it's a larger problem than most people assume. An easily solved problem, but without a solution, it is easy to see how it could generate distractions.

2. Then, one begins to abbreviate things, to look for the REAL meaning, because many things appear to be pointless or worthless. At this point, one becomes more interested in the FUNCTIONS OF THINGS. One looks for life's TRUE PURPOSE, hidden behind the ordinary. But, on a mental level, this understanding is abstract, and not really material. Things are understood through words like 'History' and 'Intentions'. The effect is not wholly clarifying.

3. Now, one might want to develop a system, but the system must be fairly perfect to qualify. Sometimes if one does invent a system, it becomes the platform for one's life. One becomes a branch on the tree of knowledge, and development partly ceases. However, for most, one enters a symbolic stage, in which one assesses if the world is significant. Sometimes this becomes an obsession with family. Other times, one is distanced from the family, and clings to feelings of pleasure, pain, or circumstance to explain reality, or to explain one's own process of discovering meaning.

4. In general (gradually) the concepts, it turns out, are inhibiting vision. One becomes tired at work because it is like physical labor. The signs one has been using do not have the power that one assumed. For some people, this is when they become depressed. And, seeing the world in an unchanging way, they take their depression as the permanent condition of the world. However, for some, the signs are still changeable, and the meaning still has life. They seek what they take to be intellectual or humanitarian employment.

Now we have followed the second ring of the dialectical circle of meditation.

The next step, if we can manage it, is to find something concrete or REAL to hold onto.

But if that is not possible, then we must confront the idea that reality may have ILLUSIONS.

1. The next thing one confronts is the opinions in one's own mind. This can be done with various degrees of rigor. Not everyone is completely relieved from nagging doubts and negative opinions. The goal, however, is to seek clarity. Those who achieve an adequate amount sometimes stop looking for more. On the other hand, some people who value clarity find very little at all. It is a period of dissatisfaction.

2. Next, one confronts the images
which one may think one under-
stands, which surround one, or
announce themselves, through
this plight in life. They may often
be psychologists, or sometimes
important friends, or objects
which do not lend their secrets
readily. At some point an insight is
granted that one has, if not understanding, then at least better understanding than before. At this
point, one begins to make progress.

3. Perhaps one felt closed up and insular, or perhaps one felt socially inadequate. Whatever the case, one has moved beyond it now. It turns out it was mental semantics. It wasn't the problematic that meant something, either to you or someone else. And it wasn't the solution, either. The solution was a matter of pride, a milestone along the path, but it wasn't everything. It wasn't even the proper thing to think about. You move on.

4. Now, either you feel adequate, or you are still yearning for something. Very often what is desired is prosperity, love, or acceptance. One becomes devoted to one's own life-project. And it is not easy going at first, but one makes tremendous progress. It feels much better than being a loner, or having nothing accomplished, or having no one to raise your hopes. What now? Could this be the end?

One enters the fourth dialectical circle. Some reach this in middle age, some reach it earlier.

It is a stage in which the individual looks for truth from other people. It is also a stage in which the person is seeking secrets to solve the snags and loose ends in their life. Sometimes people who have solved these problems simply indulge their advantages. But this may be a symptom of dishonesty. It is a time of continued uncertainty for the big questions. Much of the time, these questions are simultaneously being ignored.

1. Usually, one has problems. Problems develop over time, and often they get worse when they are not addressed. People either come to the conclusion that they need to solve their own problems, or someone else has to step in to help them out. Often it's the police, or someone giving some very strong advice. Whatever the case, one begins to look for the secrets that would prevent problematic situations from happening ever again.

2. In the middle of some of the worst things that have ever happened, you raise the gumption to ask someone for some frank advice. When you receive the advice, you feel better, and more than that, you feel better about something that was really awful to begin with. Life's motions carry you, like magic, to a better place.

3. However, you realize, that was just a PRACTICAL problem! What ever happened to the ultimate nature of life, the universe, and everything? To an older adult, this may look like a sleazy question. But the fact is, someone has to ask it, and upon reflection, why is life so unfair? Why did the glory days fade away? Is it just that what happened was the best explanation? If you're wise, you start to realize that you have your own sense of dignity, however insignificant it might be. Dignity becomes the secret key to a new level of insight. All you have to do to be immortal is have an unfinished project, theoretically!

4. Finally, you either discover that you are or you aren't a paradigm. And the paradigm's living or dead. And there was or there wasn't a problem. And you were loyal as a dog to the truth, or just didn't care. Life dishes it all back to you, and if you're doing the same thing, then you continue to live. Anyone who finds this satisfying probably has a lot of year ahead of them.

NATHAN COPPEDGE

END OF TEXT

PERPETUAL MOTION GENIUS' GUIDES

Architecture & Automobiles
Historical Deaths
Intelligent Babies
Intelligent Children
Intelligent Young Adults
Intelligent Young Poets
Interface Design
Meaning
Philosophy
Writing

OTHER SERIES BY NATHAN COPPEDGE

The Dimensional Encyclopedia

BIO

Nathan Coppedge has been quoted in Book Forum and the Hartford Courant. He is a member of the International Honor Society for philosophy. He is the author of over thirty books.